REDEEMING the TIME

STRATEGIES FOR EFFECTIVE TIME MANAGEMENT

PASTOR AMOS DADA PhD; P.Eng

International Gathering of Eagles Series

Copyright © 2023 Pastor Amos Dada PhD; P.Eng.

All rights reserved. No part of this book may be reproduced, stored, or transmitted by any means—whether auditory, graphic, mechanical, or electronic—without written permission of both publisher and author, except in the case of brief excerpts used in critical articles and reviews. Unauthorized reproduction of any part of this work is illegal and is punishable by law.

ISBN: 978-1-63950-213-4 (sc)
ISBN: 978-1-63950-214-1 (e)

This publication contains the opinions and ideas of its author. It is intended to provide helpful and informative material on the subjects addressed in the publication. The author and publisher specifically disclaim all responsibility for any liability, loss, or risk, personal or otherwise, which is incurred as a consequence, directly or indirectly, of the use and application of any of the contents of this book.

Writers Apex

Gateway Towards Success

8063 MADISON AVE #1252
Indianapolis, IN 46227
+13176596889
www.writersapex.com

www.cacbethel.com
www.igoeministry.com

CONTENTS

Foreword v

Acknowledgment ix

Dedication xi

Introduction xiii

Preface xv

Chapter 1   Understanding Time 1

Chapter 2   Watch How You Spend Time 19

Chapter 3   The Acronyms of REDEEMING TIME 47

You will never find time for anything,
if you want time you must create it.
—Charles Buxton

Your future is created by what you do today, not tomorrow.
—Anonymous.

Time is really the only capital that any human
being has, and the only thing he can't afford to lose."
—Thomas Edison

The best way to spend your time is not only to be
presence of Jesus but to proclaim the gospel of Jesus.
—Amos Dele Dada

FOREWORD

I really want to bless the name of the Lord for the inspiration of the Holy Spirit and the divine revelation that brought this book into reality.

This book, "REDEEMING THE TIME" is a book you must read; because it is without doubt God inspired, in the sense that it is based on an in-depth development of the subject which will undoubtedly lay to rest a lot of controversies on this subject. This book is also born out of an overwhelming revelation and a spontaneous spiritual inspiration.

Significance Of Time Management: This book is not just a bunch of theories but a total X-ray of the word of God coming to life through a personal experience of a life that has been transformed by God through a total adherence and dedication to the study of the scripture, and I have no doubt that it will be a blessing to everyone who will have the privilege of reading through it, and those who will be willing to submit to the word of the gospel in relation to time management.

God created time: (1) For orderliness (2) For Season - Eccl. 3:1 and (3) For Man to put their heart unto wisdom Ps 90:12

Redeeming the time - Trying to use our time judiciously because time wasted cannot be recalled. It does not mean just thinking about tomorrow. It means to use time well, accurately and judiciously. - 2 Cor. 6:2.

Meaning not letting go of whatever opportunities you have now while God's grace is still available - 2 Cor. 6:1.

Be Proactive and Make the Best Use of Every Opportunity: Biblically the Church is not an event we attend, but a family in which we participate in. The church is not somewhere we go, it is something that we are.

You are the Church! (1 Pet. 4:10). Each one should use whatever gifts he has received to serve others, faithful administering God's grace in its various forms.

Phillip made use of the opportunity to serve tables and because he was faithful in ordinary things he was assigned to become a wonder to do the miraculous. Luke 16:10 "He that is faithful in that which is least is faithful also in much...".

While God's Promises are still open to us by serving the Lord now, there is no time for procrastination. Redeem the time while your body is strong and able, while you still have that inner energy and vigor. Rom. 11:15. Surrender to him now and not later by leading your children to Christ. Ps. 32:8. Let us teach our children the word of God.

According to the author, and I quote: "The focus of this book is to assist you on how to fulfill your God desired, designed, engineered purpose through strategic and effective management of the time. One of my popular sayings is that to effectively manage our time God gave us twenty-four hours in a day. These could be divided into three 'eight hours' segments, the first eight hours to work, the next eight hours to sleep and the last eight hours to do whatever you like. The management of these last eight will determine if you shall become a billionaire or beggar.

In this book, we'll discuss some principles on how to invest your time wisely so that you can experience greater productivity in work and life based on the admonition from Paul "See then that ye walk circumspectly, not as fools, but as wise, redeeming the time, because the days are evil." Eph 5:15-16".

Knowing and considering the enormous in-depth of knowledge on this subject of Redeeming The Time, Dr. Dele Dada has done a detailed and explicit research; given the progressive and the developmental details of his work on this subject, I believe all questions and all issues of controversies have been well addressed.

Dr. Dada holds three strategic portfolios under my leadership in our mission CAC North America Latunde Region. He is the Dean, Christ Apostolic Church Noth America Bible School, the Chairman, Christ Apostolic Church Men Association (CACMA), and Zonal Superintendent Christ Apostolic Church Bethel Canada Zone. He is also the Convener of the International Gathering of Eagles Conference, another ministry that he started in 2003 that gives him opportunity to travel to several nations, sometimes up to twelve in one year teaching leadership principles and raising an eagle generation. Dr Dada has demonstrated strategies of effective time management that he shares in this book.

I have learnt a lot from this man of God as a person upon whose life is the hand of God, and this book which has really dealt with all the intricacies of time management. I therefore prayerfully and wholeheartedly recommend this book to every genuine child of God. It will stir up in you that sincere faith to put your trust in the power of God through Prayer and what prayer can do in handling the issue of Time Management. Thank you and remain blessed in Jesus name.

Pastor Timothy Akin Omolayo Agbeja, Ph.D,
Chancellor, C. A. C. North America Bible Institute,
DCC Superintendent, Christ Apostolic Church,
Washington District Co-ordinating Council, USA,
Regional Superintendent, C. A. C. North America
(Latunde Region).

ACKNOWLEDGMENT

I thank God for giving me the opportunity to be alive to write this book. Any post Covid-19 author like me should appreciate God.

I thank all my associates in the International Gathering of Eagles Network. This book is a product of the 2016 International Gathering of Eagles Conference. I appreciate all the speakers that year - Reverend Samuel Sowah (Ghana), Reverend Reggie Ephraim (India), Reverend Judy Mayes (deceased) and Bishop Audrey James (deceased); the two gospel artists, Kelvin Ambassador and Toyin Crandell.

In 2016 we also had strategic Leadership Trainings in many nations around the world. I want to thank the Pastors that hosted us in different nations. In Africa, Dr. Jim Musaka (Zimbabwe), Pastors Paul Carvalho (Angola), Binod Kumar (Nepal), Rev. Sabado Ernesto Bila (Mozambique), Pastors Adrinka Elijah (Ghana), Isaiah Dada and Adegbola Oladimeji (Nigeria). In Asian nations, Pastor Obed Oppong (China), Apostle Rodel Magalin (Philippines), Pastor Andie Padilla (Philippines), Rev. Dr. Chris & Pastor (Mrs.) Eva Akujuo (Thailand), Dr. Sam Gift and Pastor Justin (Singapore). I cannot forget our hosts in Europe, Dr. Kuyebi (Ireland), Pastors Michael Opebiyi, Soga Ogunsanu, Lawrence Folayan and Chris Oluwatubosun (England).

I want to also appreciate Pastor (Dr.) Benjamin Akinriola, my traveling partner to the Asian nations. Bishop Darrell Gooden deserves my blessings as my traveling partner to the African nations. (Read my book " Raising An Eagle Generation") In Toronto, I want to appreciate Pastors Emmanuel Ojo, Sunday Dada, Titus Owaseye, Evans Uadiale, Charles Kabowei, and David Isalana, for their help in running the conference and keeping the home front when I was away.

I want to thank ALL Bethelites in Canada zone (Toronto, Brampton, London, Windsor, Calgary, Scarborough, Virginia), and those in Nigeria, Kenya, Ghana, Uganda, Tanzania, India, and the churches under their leadership for their unflinching support for the International Gathering of Eagles Conference and vision each year.

Also, I want to acknowledge Debbie Dada for the cover design, Tosin Adegboyega for assisting with editing, and Lady Evangelist Eyitayo Dada for all she is doing to make my life beautiful, colorful and pleasant, and for editing this book and all my books with a no-nonsense approach! Finally, thank you, Pastor Dr. Timothy Akin Omolayole Agbeja, the Regional Superintendent Christ Apostolic Church North America for writing the foreword. Your life shall move forward in Jesus name.

DEDICATION

To all those who have maximized time and made a success of their lives and those that will through this book change the trajectory of their lives!

I dedicate this book to appreciate God for good health, 38 years of ministry, 37 years of blessed marriage and 20 years of International Gathering of Eagles Conference (2003-2023), the opportunity to preach the gospel in 82 nations and hold the IGOE Conference in 45 nations. Thank you, Baba God. O taste and see that the Lord is good.

Time management is Life management.
—Anonymous

Let our advance worrying become advance thinking and planning.
—Winston Churchill

Yesterday is gone. Tomorrow has not yet come.
We have only today. Let us begin.
—Mother Teresa

O taste and see that the Lord is good. I have tasted and I have seen that the Lord is good. You too can do so and even better.
—Amos Dele Dada

INTRODUCTION

If you have decided to read this book, I know you want to address time management in your life. You want to be wise with the resources and time God has given you. I want to ask for a big favour from you. Don't let this book be just "another book" in your library. By "another book," I mean a book that you will just allow to gather dust on your shelf, or a book you will read and trash to your physical or mental bin. Let this be a book that will be a reference point in your life. Let it be a book that will make you shout "Eureka!"- I found the key to redeem my time. I have found the missing key. I found the solution to my life's issues.

Miles Davis said "Time isn't the main thing, it is the only thing." Seriously, come to think of it, there is no man that does not have opportunities in life, but failure to manage time is what leads to monumental failures and regret. I don't want you to have any more moments of regret. I want you to seriously REDEEM your time, and buy back the lost years. Buy Back the Lost Chances and opportunities. Whatever you need to buy back - marriage, relationship, family, ministry; go and buy it back. Don't delay any more. Most importantly, buy back your relationship with your creator.

Come to think of it. It is a mistake to think time is going by. Time is not going. Time is here until the world ends. It is you that is going. You don't waste time. Time is infinite. You waste yourself. You are finite. It is you that grow old and die. Time doesn't. So make better use of yourself before you expire. And one of the worst things to do with time is to compare yourself to others. A cow eats grass and gets fat but if dog eats grass, it will die. Never compare yourself with others. Run your race!

We misuse our time by living in sin. This book will teach you not to live in sin. Stop giving sin fanciful names, call a spade a spade.

It is my prayer that all your wasted time and years shall be redeemed.

> *"He swallows down riches and vomits them up again; God casts them out of his belly" Job 20:15.*

This book is to help you vomit your wasted years. This book is to motivate you to pursue whatever has swallowed your life until it is recovered. Let God use this book to cast out the spirit of the wasters, procrastination, meddlesomeness, idleness, murmuring, gossiping, lack of focus and the like that has pinned you down to poverty. This book is to help purge wretchedness, wickedness, envy, anger, wild parties, idolatry, adultery, fornication, drunkenness and the like that has come into your life. Let it give you a new lease and orientation for life. Let this book usher you to a life of prosperity, peace and joy. God changes caterpillars into butterflies, sand into pearls and coal into diamonds using time and pressure. He's working on you too!

PREFACE

Time is so germane to our existence that you will think people will really value such an essential commodity but unfortunately, it is not so. People who really want to maximize their time will do anything to develop their skill in time management by reading this book irrespective of the numerous books they have read on the subject matter.

By the grace of God, we started the International Gathering of Eagles conference in 2003, to raise an eagle generation, a people of holiness, righteousness and integrity. To achieve this noble objective, we annually seek the face of God for a theme. In 2016 we were given the theme – **"Redeeming the Time."** From 2003 to 2007, we held the conference in Toronto. However, based on prophetic direction, since 2009 we have held it across the globe. In 2016 we held this conference in 12 nations namely: Canada, Angola, Zimbabwe, Ghana, Nigeria, Thailand, Singapore, Philippines, South Korea, China, Mozambique, and Nepal. The principles shared in this book were shared with leaders in those nations to the glory of God.

The focus of this book is to assist you to fulfill your God desired, designed, engineered purpose through proper management of time. One of my popular sayings is that:

> *"To effectively manage our time God gave us twenty-four hours in a day. These could be divided into three 'eight hour' segments, first eight hours to work, the next eight hours to sleep and the last eight hours to do whatever you like. The management of this last eight will determine if you shall become a billionaire or beggar."*

In this book, we'll discuss how to invest your time wisely so that you can experience greater productivity in work and life based on Paul's admonition in Ephesians 5:15-16,

> *"See then that ye walk circumspectly, not as fools, but as wise, [16]Redeeming the time, because the days are evil."*

In Chapter One, the focus is to help you understand the terminology time, time in *"Xponoz"* (Chronological order, Chronos) and as *"Kanox"* (moments of opportunity, Kairos)- and what it means to "redeem time."

In Chapter Two, the focus is to help you understand how to manage your time.

Chapter Three, focuses on skills for time management using my acronym of 'REDEEM' and 'TIME.'

I urge you to prayerfully read this book because principles don't work where principalities are working. Follow these three wisdom keys, wisdom is knowing what to do (you want to maximize your time), skill is knowing how to do it (this book will teach you skills), and virtue is doing it. It is up to you to apply it.

Just imagine going to the grocery store to buy oranges, you peel it, slice it, but if you never put it in your mouth- you cannot enjoy it or access the necessary vitamins you need from it. Apply these principles to your life.

Pastor Amos Dada PhD; P.Eng
July 2023.

CHAPTER ONE

UNDERSTANDING TIME

See then that ye walk circumspectly, not as fools, but as wise,16 Redeeming the time, because the days are evil Eph 5:16 (KJV)

Be very careful, then, how you live—not as unwise but as wise, 16 making the most of every opportunity, because the days are evil. Eph 5:16 (NIV)

So be careful how you act; these are difficult days. Don't be fools; be wise: make the most of every opportunity you have for doing good. Eph 5: 16 (LB)

God invented Time

From the very beginning, God wanted us to be aware of the passing of time.

In Genesis God said,

"There was evening, there was morning, the first day. There was evening, there was morning the second day. And He put up in the sky, the sun and the moon and the stars."

It says in Genesis 1:14, time is:

> "To mark seasons and days and years."

Since that time, using the creativity God gave us, we have developed various time-keeping devices, like smartphones, clocks, calendars to mention a few that let us know the day, month or year. Early on, there were sundials, which would trace the movement of a shadow across the face, then Egyptians invented water clocks, the Chinese invented candle clocks. About 100 or 200 years before Christ, someone in Alexandria invented the hourglass, so dry sand, very fine sand, moving down through a neck in place in the glass and flowing down (see the cover page), so there's a sense of, "How many more grains of sand are left in my life?" Or how much is left in the day? Mechanical clocks really came in when something called an escapement, which is a sprocket, or something like that, which would rock back and forth and it enabled accurate mechanical time-keeping. God invented time for a purpose.

What is Time?

Time is an observed phenomenon, by which human beings' sense and record changes in the environment and in the universe. A literal definition is elusive. Time has been called an illusion, a dimension, a smooth-flowing continuum, and an expression of separation among events that occur in the same physical location.

According to Myles Monroe:

> "Time is an interruption of eternity. Time is a measure of eternity. Time is a piece of eternity. Time is a slice of forever. Time is a limited period during which an action or process exists and takes place. Time is the measure of space. Time is the passing of existence."

Time - it is one commodity we all have whether you are a billionaire or a beggar yet, time is a strange commodity. We can't save it, retrieve it, relive it, stretch it, recycle it, borrow it, loan it, share it, stop it, store it, or recall it, we can only use it or lose it. We can't call timeouts in the game of life.

According to the Apostle Paul, in the Greek language there are two words that are used for time; "chronos (χρόνος)" and "Kairos (καιρός)". "Chronos" is the root word for 'chronology' or 'chronological', which talks about a measure of time. Chronos (used 54 times in the New Testament) refers to a specific amount of time, such as a day or an hour (e.g. Acts 13:18 and 27:9). When you are 20, 30, or 50 years old, it means you have occupied a space for 20, 30, or 50 years. A watch tells us what 'chronos' is. When you are celebrating 50 years of age, you are dwelling in the chronology of time. Paul used the word 'Kairos' in Ephesians 5:16. Kairos speaks about opportunities; moments-open doors. Kairos (used 86 times in the New Testament) refers to an opportune time, a "moment" or a "season" such as "harvest time" Kairos speaks about what you do with chronos. That is what you fill your age with- what you fill the 20, 30, or 50 year span of your life with. It speaks of "buying the time"- buy the opportunity this time has presented to you.

There are things you must do at this moment that you can never do tomorrow if you don't do it now. If you are to pray now for ten minutes for someone not to die but you postpone it and the person dies later in the day - even if you pray for ten hours tomorrow to procure that miracle, it is an abuse of time. It is meaningless.

What does it mean to Redeem?

The bible says that we should,

> "Count our days that we might apply our hearts to wisdom."

The word 'redeem' can be broken into two words. 'Deem' means own; 're' means redo, put together, 'redeem' means re-own, buy the time back, the time you have misused. To redeem means to re-own or re-control time, repossess time, to fulfill a pledge or promise, convert into value and to pay an outstanding debt to deliver on a commitment. Let me explain what it means to 'redeem' using two kings in the Old Testament- Ahaz and Hezekiah.

> *2 Chronicles 28:1-2; 27*
> ¹*Ahaz was twenty years old when he became king, and he reigned in Jerusalem for sixteen years. He did not do what was pleasing in the sight of the Lord, as his ancestor David had done.* ²*Instead, he followed the example of the kings of Israel. He cast metal images for the worship of Baal.*
>
> ²⁷*When Ahaz died, he was buried in Jerusalem but not in the royal cemetery of the kings of Judah. Then his son Hezekiah became the next king.*
>
> *2 Chronicles 29:1-3*
> ¹*Hezekiah was twenty-five years old when he became the king of Judah, and he reigned in Jerusalem twenty-nine years. His mother was Abijah, the daughter of Zechariah.* ²*He did what was pleasing in the Lord's sight, just as his ancestor David had done.* ³*In the very first month of the first year of his reign, Hezekiah reopened the doors of the Temple of the Lord and repaired them.*
>
> *2 Chronicles 32:33*
> ³³*And Hezekiah slept with his fathers, and they buried him in the chiefest (upper area) of the sepulchers of the sons of David: and all Judah and the inhabitants of Jerusalem did him honour at his death. And Manasseh his son reigned in his stead.*

These stories show that Ahaz misused his 'chronos'. He did not use the time in a way that honoured God and based on that, when he died, they refused to bury him with the royals. On the other hand, Hezekiah put good decisions into his 'chronos' that made the people not just bury him in the royal sepulcher, but the special area of the sepulcher. The founding father of Christ Apostolic Church, Joseph Ayo Babalola, did great work with his 'chronos.' He was not only buried in a physical place that was honorable, his works live on. The man who did not complete Grade 12 diploma or School Certificate now has a university Joseph Ayo Babalola University (JABU) named after him.

Time is tied to opportunity.

An ancient Greek statue depicted a man with wings on his feet, a large lock of hair on the front of his head, and no hair at all on the back. Beneath was the inscription:

> *"Who made thee?*
> > *Lysippos made me.*
> *What is thy name?*
> > *My name is OPPORTUNITY.*
> *Why hast thou wings on thy feet?*
> > *That I may fly away swiftly.*
> *Why hast thou a great forelock?*
> > *That men may seize me when I come.*
> *Why art thou bald in the back?*
> > *That when I am gone by, none can lay hold of me."*

To redeem time is to seize the opportunity to use time judiciously.

Some Misconceptions about Time:

1. "I just need to buy some time."

Did you know that with all the money in the world you cannot even buy a moment of time?

In the Bible there is a story about a man called Lazarus (John 11). Lazarus was dead for four days. Jesus came and raised him up from the dead. Jesus redeemed Lazarus' time.

In the Bible there is a story about a woman who had spent all the money she had because she was sick and weak because she had uncontrolled bleeding (Luke 8:43-48). All the money she had could not stop the bleeding, could not make her well, could not give her the badly needed strength to go on. But when she heard about Jesus, her faith began to build. She struggled with all of her might to get close enough to Jesus, simply to touch the hem of His garment. You see, she could not buy time, but she touched the hem of God's garment and was healed. God controls our time; we cannot buy it.

2. "I think I will make a little time."

Do you remember the Bible story of the fool who saw how plentiful his crop was and decided to build bigger barns? (Luke 12:16-21)

> *18 And he said, This will I do: I will pull down my barns, and build greater; and there will I bestow all my fruits and my goods.*

He is a fool because he had no God in his agenda. Jesus called him a fool because his life was going to be taken from him that night. It reminds me of a young man who died recently. He just slept and did not wake up. He had a fantastic job, great wife and beautiful children. Everything seemed to be going well, but a heart attack came. Who knows who is next? If we could make time, I am sure we would, but it is a Him-possibility. That's right, Him! God makes time, we can't.

3. "I need to make up for LOST time."

Friend, there is nothing we can do about the time that has already passed. No permutation or arithmetic can bring 2022 back! I know we all have regrets. We have not used our time as wisely as we should have.

I wish there was something I could do about all the time I have wasted doing unprofitable things. "I could have," "I would have," "I should have,"- are all regrets. But there is only one thing we can do, and that's to use the time we have left wisely.

4. "I don't have time. I am busy!"

It reminds me about the story of a man who was always saying "I am busy." He was invited to church but he never went. Then he died and appeared at the judgment seat of God. Then God searched the book of life and said, "I remember you, but I guess I was too busy to write your name in the book of life!"

I remember another story. When we just arrived in Canada, one of our daughters was in day care and my wife told her teacher that I was a pastor. She took interest in us and said that her husband used to be a pastor and would like to meet me. Days passed by, turning to months and each time I asked her about her husband, she would say "Oh, he is very busy." One day, she told me her husband was in the hospital. I said jokingly "No it is not possible, he is too busy to be in the hospital." She pleaded that I should pay him a visit and pray with him. I did it with my mum. God healed him instantly. He promised to see me after leaving the hospital. Once again, he was too busy. Not quite six months later, the wife told me her husband had died! You have time for the things that are most important to you. It is not that you don't have time to attend services, bible studies and prayer meetings; it is that you do not make it a priority. When you don't want to do something, you find excuses. Someone once said:

"If you wait for all green lights, you'll never get going."

How true that is! You have time left, the question is, "What are your top priorities? That is where you will spend your time. Like money, where your treasure is, that is where your heart will be.

I think it is time to redeem the time!

Purpose of Time

Purpose gives birth to dreams, ignites your talents, generates passion, protects you from failures and is the basis of success. In the words of Dr. Myles Munroe of blessed memory, "When the purpose of a thing (or person) is unknown, abuse is inevitable."

On a lighter note, the purpose of time was defined by a boy that was having a conversation with his father:

> Dad to son: "Son, do you know that I have been thinking about the purpose of time since I was a little kid your age." His son kept on licking his ice cream.
>
> "And you know what I have learned after all these years."
>
> "Umm." his son says, licking his ice cream.
>
> "That we should stop asking this stupid question and enjoy the ice cream before it melts." and then he starts licking his ice cream.

I think what the boy insinuates is that the purpose of time is to use it now and use it appropriately.

A physicist defined the purpose of time on an intellectual level saying "the greatest mystery about time is that it flows." Physics considers it as another dimension of space, but it is quite different from space. Pick any coordinate system and you can sit still in space, but not time. That effect is currently ignored in physics. Some theorists draw the conclusion that because the flow of time isn't currently included in physics theories, therefore the movement of time isn't real, but is an illusion. Physics is supposed to account for reality, not deny it! Some people claim that the progress of time is related to entropy, but that argument does not hold up under scrutiny. The only theory that makes sense is that the progress of time derives from cosmology.

To the ordinary man like you and I, the purpose of time is to measure the existence of life - to define life. It takes utilization of time to define purpose. The purpose of time is to measure the quality of time - to account for your life; to define the distance between your beginning and your end; to live life in doses; to measure the purpose of life.

X.J. Kennedy said "The Purpose of Time is to Prevent Everything from Happening at Once." From that we can deduce that the purpose of time is to give you 'space' to do something or not do it. Without time you will not have time to do anything. To write this book I need time to express myself on my computer, or verbally and allow technology to translate it to words for me. A person unborn cannot talk about time or its purpose. Talking about the purpose of time is highly philosophical.

The Bible Encourages us to Maximize Time.

The purpose of this book is not just to recharge our intellectual capacity or accumulate knowledge but to help you use the little time you have on earth and use it well. That is why the Psalmist says:

> *"So teach us to number our days, that we may apply our hearts unto wisdom." Psalm 90:12 (KJV)*

> *Lord, make me to know mine end, and the measure of my days, what it is: that I may know how frail I am. Psalm 39:4 (KJV)*

Job also referred to the purpose of time and its limitation:

> *[5]"A person's days are determined; you have decreed the number of his months and have set limits he cannot exceed. [6] So look away from him and let him alone, till he has put in his time like a hired laborer." Job 14:5-6 (NIV)*

Solomon, the man acknowledged to be a man of wisdom, said:

> *"¹For everything there is a season, a time for every activity under heaven. ²A time to be born and a time to die. A time to plant and a time to harvest. ³A time to kill and a time to heal. A time to tear down and a time to build up. ⁴A time to cry and a time to laugh. A time to grieve and a time to dance. ⁵A time to scatter stones and a time to gather stones. A time to embrace and a time to turn away. ⁶A time to search and a time to quit searching. A time to keep and a time to throw away. ⁷A time to tear and a time to mend. A time to be quiet and a time to speak. ⁸A time to love and a time to hate. A time for war and a time for peace." Ecclesiastes 3:1-8 (NIV)*

> *"For there is a proper time and procedure for every matter, though a person may be weighed down by misery." Ecclesiastes 8:6 (NIV)*

Solomon is speaking about the two meanings of time. He is telling you to count the number of your days numerically or chronologically but more than anything package wisdom into the way you are using it. Apply wisdom to the way you are using time because if you don't, you make a mockery of it.

It is sad to note that Solomon himself failed to maximize time on earth. He put wrong things into his Chronos for the Bible says:

> *"But King Solomon loved many strange women, together with the daughter of Pharaoh, women of the Moabites, Ammonites, Edomites, Zidonians, and Hittites:*
>
> *²Of the nations concerning which the Lord said unto the children of Israel, Ye shall not go in to them, neither shall they come in unto you: for surely they will turn away your heart after their gods: Solomon clave unto these in love. ³And he had seven hundred wives, princesses, and*

> *three hundred concubines: and his wives turned away his heart. ⁴For it came to pass, when Solomon was old, that his wives turned away his heart after other gods: and his heart was not perfect with the Lord his God, as was the heart of David his father. ⁵For Solomon went after Ashtoreth the goddess of the Zidonians, and after Milcom the abomination of the Ammonites. ⁶And Solomon did evil in the sight of the Lord, and went not fully after the Lord, as did David his father."*

What are you chasing after? What is derailing your life? What is making you to loose focus? Solomon got distracted by women and wealth.

I pray that you will learn from Solomon. It is one thing to have knowledge, it is another thing to use knowledge. This type of issue is what I call the pain of God.

The Pain of God

One of the greatest pains of God is to see people misuse their time and waste great opportunities he has given them. That is why Paul warned us not to be fools. A fool is someone with poor judgment or little intelligence. He is self-opinionated, unwilling to learn or be corrected, talks too much, having no self-control, gossiping, not planning ahead, meddling in the matters of others, quick to respond, stubborn, lazy, stingy, putting hope in money, despising father's instructions and so on. Examples abound in the bible of people who misused their time and God was so thoroughly displeased that he sanctioned and allowed terrible things to happen to them. Let us look at the cases of Adam, Samson, Eli and David.

Adam

Do you know why God came to the earth physically in Genesis chapter three? Only Adam was in human form on earth. That was the only time

God came to the earth to check on men. When men started behaving like fools, he stopped coming physically and started to send men to meet men.

> "⁸When the cool evening breezes were blowing, the man and his wife heard the Lord God walking about in the garden. So they hid from the Lord God among the trees. ⁹Then the Lord God called to the man, "Where are you?" ¹⁰He replied, "I heard you walking in the garden, so I hid. I was afraid because I was naked." Genesis 3:8-10 (NLT)

Adam was so foolish that he was hiding from God. Before you judge Adam, remember this book is not to judge Adam; rather it is for you to learn from Adam. Are you hiding from God? Some people will not come to church because they committed sin - that is hiding from God. Some don't just hide when they are confronted with an issue in their lives; they blame others like Adam blamed Eve. Adam misused the opportunity of transforming the garden of Eden. There is a garden God has given you: marital garden, business garden, ministerial garden; use it well. Redeem the time.

Beyond that he also led humanity in the way of sin. Don't be a fool by committing sin or leading your family and your generation in the way of sin.

Samson

God did not come down to personally correct Samson in his foolishness. He did not send someone beyond his parents to warn him of his foolishness. He allowed his foolishness to consume him. He allowed the enemy to teach him the lesson on how not to be foolish. Maybe you are a young man or woman reading this book and your parents are warning you about how and whom to marry and you are already behaving foolishly. Don't do it.

> *"One day when Samson was in Timnah, one of the Philistine women caught his eye. ²When he returned home, he told his father and mother, "A young Philistine woman in Timnah caught my eye. I want to marry her. Get her for me." ³His father and mother objected. "Isn't there even one woman in our tribe or among all the Israelites you could marry?" they asked. "Why must you go to the pagan Philistines to find a wife?" Judge 14:1-3 (NLT).*

It is not only that Samson behaved foolishly in not listening to sound advice; he refused to grow in wisdom.

But Samson told his father, "Get her for me! She looks good to me." Samson spent his days and years pursuing women instead of Judging Israel.

Samson made the same mistake Eve made - 'it looks good to the eye.' Many make foolish decisions based on what they see. As students we say - stop committing *"lookery"*. Don't cause God pain by what you see. Think before you act.

When God gives you an opportunity and you fail you cause God pain.

David

When David behaved foolishly by committing adultery, God sent a man named Prophet Nathan.

> *"Then Nathan said to David, "You are that man! The Lord, the God of Israel, says: I anointed you king of Israel and saved you from the power of Saul. ⁸I gave you your master's house and his wives and the kingdoms of Israel and Judah. And if that had not been enough, I would have given you much, much more. ⁹Why, then, have you despised the word of the Lord and done this horrible deed? For you have murdered Uriah the Hittite with the sword of the*

> *Ammonites and stolen his wife. ¹⁰From this time on, your family will live by the sword because you have despised me by taking Uriah's wife to be your own. ¹¹"This is what the Lord says: Because of what you have done, I will cause your own household to rebel against you. I will give your wives to another man before your very eyes, and he will go to bed with them in public view. ¹² You did it secretly, but I will make this happen to you openly in the sight of all Israel."*
> *2 Samuel 12: 7-12 (NLT)*

When David was supposed to be at war front he was at home engaging in unwholesome affair with Bathsheba. Similarly, you caused God pain when instead of championing and propagating the gospel through witnessing, but rather you are engaging in fornication, adultery, rape, assault, womanizing, watching pornography and engaging in all manner of sexual perversions.

God loves you and goes all out to show it by choosing you above your brethren, but when you sin like David it is a foolish act. Sin is a reproach. David caused God pain, he acted foolishly and paid for it dearly. Learn from others' mistakes, not your own.

Eli

When Eli misbehaved, God sent a prophet to him and later Samuel.

> *"One day a man of God came to Eli and gave him this message from the Lord: "I revealed myself to your ancestors when they were Pharaoh's slaves in Egypt. ²⁸I chose your ancestor Aaron[i] from among all the tribes of Israel to be my priest, to offer sacrifices on my altar, to burn incense, and to wear the priestly vest as he served me. And I assigned the sacrificial offerings to you priests. ²⁹So why do you scorn my sacrifices and offerings? Why do you give your sons more honor than you give me—for you and they have*

> *become fat from the best offerings of my people Israel!* ³⁰ *"Therefore, the Lord, the God of Israel, says: I promised that your branch of the tribe of Levi would always be my priests. But I will honor those who honor me, and I will despise those who think lightly of me.* ³¹ *The time is coming when I will put an end to your family, so it will no longer serve as my priests. All the members of your family will die before their time. None will reach old age.* ³² *You will watch with envy as I pour out prosperity on the people of Israel. But no members of your family will ever live out their days.* ³³ *The few not cut off from serving at my altar will survive, but only so their eyes can go blind and their hearts break, and their children will die a violent death.* ³⁴ *And to prove that what I have said will come true, I will cause your two sons, Hophni and Phinehas, to die on the same day!* 1 Samuel 2: 27-34 (NLT).

You don't want the kind of harsh decision that God made regarding Eli and his family to be your portion? Don't cause God pain out of your foolishness. Redeem the time.

What it Means to Redeem Time

The context of the command to redeem the time in Ephesians helps us understand what redeeming the time looks like and why it's important.

> *"Be careful how you live. Don't live like fools, but like those who are wise. Make the most of every opportunity in these evil days. Don't act thoughtlessly but understand what the Lord wants you to do. Don't be drunk with wine, because that will ruin your life"* Ephesians 5:15-18 (NLT).

Redeeming the time means that we are careful about how we live. We seek out and employ wisdom (see Proverbs 2:1-15). We seize every opportunity and use it for God's glory. We think through our plans and make sure they align with God's will, and we avoid empty, harmful activities such as getting drunk. Why are we to live this way? "Because the days are evil." (Ephesians 5:16). We must overcome evil with good (Romans 12:21).

Jesus taught His disciples the necessity of redeeming the time:

> *"We must work the works of him who sent me while it is day; night is coming, when no one can work"* John 9:4 (ESV).

Jesus was diligent about keeping to His mission. Distractions were as prevalent then as they are now, but He did not let any of them deter Him from preaching and teaching God's Word and most importantly for dying on the cross. They wanted to make him earthly king, he preferred to reign as heavenly king. That was why He came (Luke 4:43). Though He spent only thirty three and half years on this earth, Jesus changed the world forever because He redeemed the time.

We can learn to redeem the time by becoming conscious of the fact that we may not have another day. The song "Live Like You Were Dying" by Tim McGraw is about redeeming the time. While its focus is on pursuing earthly passions in the time we have left, the lyrics make an important point. They conclude with this thought: "Someday I hope you get the chance to live like you were dying." As Christians, we should live like we're dying and pursue all God has given us to do while we have time. Everything done for Christ on earth earns eternal rewards (Mark 9:41). Things that are done for selfish, carnal reasons will burn up and be blown away (1 Corinthians 3:12-15).

Another way we can learn to redeem time is by asking God to help us. We should start every morning by committing our day to the Lord and asking Him to help us do something that day that has eternal significance. By beginning our day with eternity in mind, we become more aware of spiritual nudges in our hearts. We look for ways we can honor the Lord, help someone else, or utilize our time in productive ways. Sitting at a red light, we can pray for our neighbor. Mopping the floor, we can worship in song. At a restaurant, we can leave an extra big tip along with a gospel tract or a card inviting the waiter to church. We can evaluate our gifts and interests and find ways to invest them for God's kingdom. Volunteering, serving at church, leading a ministry, taking Bible studies to the jails and prisons, and studying to show ourselves "approved unto God" are all ways we can redeem the time (2 Timothy 2:15).

James 4:14 Reminds us that our earthly lives are no more than a fog that appears and then quickly evaporates. Our money and possessions will be given to someone else. Our jobs will be filled by others. Our families may remember us with fondness but will move on with lives that don't include us. All that remains of our lives on earth is that which was invested in eternity. In the end, all that matters is what we did or did not do to redeem the time (Psalm 102:3; 144:4).

How do you know a fool?

The fool says in his heart, "God does not exist." They are corrupt; they do vile deeds. There is no one who does good. Psalm 14:1. Anyone that denies God's existence either based on philosophical or evolutionary thinking or for any reason is a fool. Anyone that disdains God, makes mockery of God, fails to serve God, queries God's judgment with their feeble and microscopic knowledge is a fool. Anyone not living for God fully even if he/she goes to church is a fool. Fools are proud, pretentious, uncaring and at times at their peril. It's a dangerous thing to join the company of fools. Fools despite the knowledge of God available in our generations and if they fail to repent they will go to hell. Don't be part of that. Fools are known for their failure to apply knowledge appropriately. My illustration has always been, everyone has knowledge, the problem is application. No matter how solid a place looks - when they warn the wise man that there is a hole he should avoid walking on it. But a fool will tell you it's not possible and fall into it. Otherwise how do you explain a medical doctor that teaches that smoking kills yet smokes like a chimney!

Beloved, don't play the fool. This year, learn to walk with the wise so that you can be wise. Make necessary amends and do not repeat those mistakes that led you into previous problems. One Yoruba proverb says "B'omode ba subu a wo'waju, b'agba ba subu a wehin wo." It means, "when a kid falls he looks at the front, but when an adult falls, he looks back." Remember where you have fallen, says Jesus to the backsliding church in Ephesus, and follow Apostle Paul's exhortation "See then that you walk circumspectly, not as fools but as wise". Always remember that "The fear of the Lord is the beginning of wisdom. Stay safe, stay upright.

CHAPTER TWO

WATCH HOW YOU SPEND TIME

¹But know this, that in the last days perilous times will come: ²For men will be lovers of themselves, lovers of money, boasters, proud, blasphemers, disobedient to parents, unthankful, unholy, ³unloving, unforgiving, slanderers, without self-control, brutal, despisers of good, ⁴traitors, headstrong, haughty, lovers of pleasure rather than lovers of God, ⁵having a form of godliness but denying its power. And from such people turn away! ⁶For of this sort are those who creep into households and make captives of gullible women loaded down with sins, led away by various lusts, ⁷always learning and never able to come to the knowledge of the truth ⁸Now as Jannes and Jambres resisted Moses, so do these also resist the truth: men of corrupt minds, disapproved concerning the faith; ⁹but they will progress no further, for their folly will be manifest to all, as theirs also was. 2 Timothy 3:1-9 (NKJV).

Why time management matters?

Many people have spoken across the ages, nations, cultures and continents, regarding the subject of time as follows:

"Time is the school in which we learn, time is the fire in which we burn."

—Delmore Schwartz

"Ordinary people think merely of spending time. Great people think of using it."

—Author unknown

"You're writing the story of your life one moment at a time."

—Doc Childre and Howard Martin

"Lost time is never found again."

—Proverb

"All that really belongs to us is time; even he who has nothing else has that."

—Baltasar Gracian

"Time is at once the most valuable and the most perishable of all our possessions."

—John Randolph

"Time is really the only capital that any human being has, and the only thing he can't afford to lose."

—Thomas Edison

"The great dividing line between success and failure can be expressed in five words: 'I did not have time.'"

—Franklin Field

"Until we can manage time, we can manage nothing else."

—Peter F. Druck

Amasis The Egyptian King

Amasis II or Ahmose II was a Pharaoh (reigned 570 – 526 BCE) of the Twenty-sixth Dynasty of Egypt, the successor of Apries at Sais. He was the last great ruler of Egypt before the Persian conquest.

Amasis taught humanity about strategic effective time management. One of the stories about him states: In the early morning, and until the time of the filling of the market he did with a good will the business which was brought before him; but after this he passed the time jesting at his boon-companions and was frivolous and playful. And his friends being troubled at it admonished him in some such words as these: "O king, thou dost not rightly govern thyself in thus letting thyself descend to behavior so trifling; for thou oughtest rather to have been sitting throughout the day stately upon a stately throne and administering thy business; and so the Egyptians would have been assured that they were ruled by a great man, and thou wouldest have had a better report: but as it is, thou art acting by no means in a kingly fashion." And he answered them thus: "They who have bows stretch them at such time as they wish to use them, and when they have finished using them, they lose them again; for if they were stretched tight always they would break, so that the men would not be able to use them when they needed them. So also, is the state of man: if he should always be in earnest and not relax himself for sport at the due time, he would either go mad or be struck with stupor before he was aware; and knowing this well, I distribute a portion of the time to each of the two ways of living." Thus he replied to his friends:

In the reign of Amasis it is said that Egypt became more prosperous than at any other time before, both in regard to that which comes to the land from the river and in regard to that which comes from the land to its inhabitants, and that at this time the inhabited towns in it numbered in all twenty thousand.

It was Amasis too who established the law that every year each one of the Egyptians should declare to the ruler of his district, from what source he got his livelihood, and if any man did not do this or did not make a declaration of an honest way of living, he should be punished with death. Now Solon the Athenian received from Egypt this law and had it enacted for the Athenians, and they have continued to observe it, since it is a law with which none can find fault.

Amasis once made an order that every man should once a year give a particular account of how he spent his time, and in what way he lived.

> *"My brethren, there is a day coming when you must all give an account of your time; all your time must be reckoned for at the great and general audit of the world." Rom 14:12*

> *For we must all appear before the judgment seat of Christ, so that each of us may receive what is due us for the things done while in the body, whether good or bad. 2 Cor 5:10*

> *"And just as it is appointed for people to die once—and after this, judgment" Heb 9:27*

"Don't Waste Your Life." - John Piper

In John Piper's book, "Desiring God" he shares a powerful memory from his days traveling with his father, who was, among other things, a traveling Evangelist. His father went from church to church and they would do revival services following that style, and pattern, and there would be a very, very clear, powerful preaching of the Gospel. There was one time that stuck out in John Piper's memory, where there had been a particularly notorious, hard-hearted, elderly man whose family and friends had been praying for years that he would come to faith in Christ. Finally, to the amazement of everyone, this man accepted Christ after hearing the Gospel clearly explained by John Piper's father, and with tears, repentance and brokenness, he received forgiveness of sins and came to faith. It was just an amazingly powerful moment.

Something crashed in on this elderly gentleman with vivid reality, and he began to realize how many years he had resisted people coming to him with the Gospel, how many family members he had turned away, how many times he had said no, and all of the years that had been wasted, "walking in vanity and pride," as the hymn puts it. As he thought about the years of his life that he had wasted, he began crying out from the bottom of his heart- "I've wasted it, I've wasted my life."

My father in-law Barrister Olajide Awoyemi told me a similar story how he was privileged to lead a very popular Yoruba politician who was known for diabolical powers to Christ at old age and how the man was full of regrets for not knowing Christ earlier.

The Resolves of Jonathan Edward

When I was in the university about forty-two years ago and I read the sermon turned into a mini book- "Sinners in the hand of an angry God" by Jonathan Edward - I have not ceased to admire his personality. Since mentors are not just those living, I can tell you Dr Martin Luther King Jr and Jonathan Edward are my mentors. You needed to see my delight at a point when I visited Yale University and saw that a hall was named after him. I took pictures in the hall like a baby!

I reproduced some of goals (resolutions) of the great preacher Jonathan Edwards, written before Edwards was 20 years old:

> *'Being sensible that I am unable to do anything without God's help, I do humbly entreat Him, by His grace, to enable me to keep these Resolutions, so far as they are agreeable to His will.'*

#1 - Resolved, that I will do whatsoever I think to be most to the glory of God, and my own good, profit, and pleasure... To do whatever I think to be my duty... for the good and advantage of mankind in general.

#4 - Resolved, Never to do any manner of thing, whether in soul or body less or more, but what tends to the glory of God...'

#5 - Resolved, Never to lose one moment of time, but to improve it in the most profitable way I possibly can.

#6 - Resolved, To live with all my might, while I do live.

#7 - Resolved, Never to do anything, which I should be afraid to do if it were the last hour of my life.

#28 - Resolved, To study the Scriptures so steadily, constantly, and frequently, as that I may find, and plainly perceive, myself to grow in the knowledge of the same.

#43 - Resolved, Never, henceforward, till I die, to act as if I were any way my own, but entirely and altogether God's.

#46 - Resolved, Never to allow the least measure of any fretting or uneasiness at my father or mother.

#70 - Resolved, (That) there be something of benevolence in all I speak. - (Edwards resolved to read these resolutions over once a week!).

Comparison of Jonathan Edwards with Max Jukes
Jonathan Edwards

Jonathan Edwards was a Puritan Preacher in the 1700s. He was one of the most respected preachers of his time. He attended Yale at the age of thirteen and later went on to become the president of Princeton College. He married his wife Sara in 1727 and they were blessed with eleven children. Every night when Mr. Edwards was home, he would spend an hour conversing with his family and then praying a blessing over each child. Jonathan and his wife Sarah passed on a great, godly legacy to their eleven children.

An American educator, A.E. Winship decided to trace the descendants of Jonathan Edwards almost 150 years after his death. His findings were remarkable, especially when compared to another man from the same time period known as Max Jukes.

Jonathan Edwards' legacy includes: 1 U.S. Vice-President, 1 Dean of a law school, 1 dean of a medical school, 3 U.S. Senators, 3 governors, 3 mayors, 13 college presidents, 30 judges, 60 doctors, 65 professors, 75 Military officers, 80 public office holders, 100 lawyers, 100 clergymen, and 285 college graduates.

How may this be explained? Edwards was a godly man, but he was also hard working, intelligent and moral. Furthermore, Winship states, "Much of the capacity and talent, intensity and character of the more than 1,400 of Edwards' family is due to Mrs. Edwards."

Max Jukes

Max Jukes' legacy came to people's attention when the family trees of 42 different men in the New York prison system were traced back to him. He lived in New York at about the same period as Edwards. The Jukes family originally was studied by sociologist Richard L. Dugdale in 1877.

Jukes' descendants included: 7 murderers, 60 thieves, 190 prostitutes, 150 other convicts, 310 paupers, and 440 who were physically wrecked by addiction to alcohol. Of the 1,200 descendants that were studied, 300 died prematurely.

These contrasting legacies provide an example of what some call the five-generation rule. "How a parent raises their child — the love they give, the values they teach, the emotional environment they offer, the education they provide — influences not only their children but the four generations to follow, either for good or evil." What a challenging thought! If someone studied your descendants four generations later, what would you want them to discover? Do you want an Edwards' legacy or a Jukes' legacy? The life you live will determine the legacy you leave. There is no doubt that the resolve of Jonathan Edward paid off. Can you duplicate that or even improve on it? I think so.

The Days are Evil

'The days are evil.' Paul admonishes us to redeem the time because the days are evil. "Evil" in the Greek means "hurtful evil in effect, calamitous, diseased, derelict and vicious." These adjectives describe our modern world, as seen in daily news headlines.

Paul says - Time can be abused.

In the opening scripture (2 Timothy 3), Paul with his spiritual binoculars saw into the future of humanity. Times are evil because we put wrong stuff into it - eg. Crime, pornography, murder (you steal time/life from somebody). The LGBT community – a tiny, microscopic number of people are derailing the world. Though they say the majority carries the vote- how come the minority are dictating the pace?

Many nations have legalized same-sex marriage. Canada is one of them. Few years ago the government also legalize cannabis which has led many young people today to suffer from mental health issues an abuse of our time.

Men are abusing time, putting wrong things into time. In Afghanistan, the Taliban are terrorizing the world. In Nigeria Boko Haram, bandits, kidnappers, Fulani herdsmen are terrorizing the world . In North

America Christian are persecuted. Vladimir Putin has destroyed Ukraine. Perilous times are indeed here. How many youths are putting cocaine, heroine, drug, alcohol into their lives? When you sleep around, move around in the company of derelict, you are abusing your body and your future. When you drop out of school, you mortgage your career. When you do not commit yourself to something noble and great, you are damaging and wasting destiny. What are you putting into time? Time is a currency like money; you can spend it; time can be stolen, lost, abused, squandered, misused, depreciated, and devalued. You can turn around today and refuse to abuse your time.

Why Must We Redeem Time?

Jonathan Edwards gives us ten reasons to redeem time:

1. The inestimable value of time.
2. The brevity and uncertainty of it.
3. The impossibility of recalling it.
4. The purpose and design of God entrusting us with it.
5. The account we must give for it.
6. Redeem the time, for time is very precious.
7. Redeem the time on account of the momentous consequences which depend on our use of it.
8. Redeem the time, for the time is short.
9. Redeem the time, for when it is once past it cannot be recovered.
10. Redeem the time, because it is not our own. Alas it is borrowed!

How Do I Redeem Time?

Invest Time

You invest your time in something. Put your time, effort, or energy into a project. Time is our most valuable resource. We can't get it back once it's gone, so we need to make sure that we invest our time wisely. Only you are in command of how you invest time. And we must learn how to utilize this important asset if we want to be productive in our work and lives. How do you invest time? I always ask myself what am I doing now and what do I need to do in the hour? I don't want an idle moment. If I have nothing to do, I will go and sleep. When I wake up there will be much more to do! Friend, at the end of each day you must ask yourself what did I do today?

Set Goals And Create A Plan To Achieve Them

One of the best ways to invest your time wisely is by setting goals and creating a plan to achieve them. When you're committed to achieving specific goals, you'll focus your efforts on what's important and avoid wasting your precious time. To create a plan, break down your goal into smaller steps that you can complete over a period of time. For example, if you want to save money, your steps might be to create a budget, track your expenses, and find ways to reduce spending.

Create Routines

Another way to invest your time wisely is by creating a routine. Most people find this boring and monotonous. But investing time in creating routines will pay off in the long run. Having a routine helps you manage your tasks every day, and week. It can also help you automate tasks that are less impactful, saving you time. Some things to consider adding to your routine include: meal planning, exercise, time for yourself, getting enough sleep, taking breaks like Ammsi of Egypt. Bishop Oyedepo said,

> *"If you don't rest, you will soon be laid to rest."*

God, in his goodness, created rest because he considers it as important as work. A loving shepherd makes sure his sheep get enough rest to stay healthy. If you won't lie down, God will make you lie down. It's also important to take breaks throughout the day. When you take short breaks, you can refresh your mind and come back to work with more energy. While in boarding house in high school in the 70s, siesta was compulsory. It has not left me, if I want to maximize my evening, I must take a nap in the day. This is key to avoiding burnout. There is something called *The Law of diminishing returns*. You can fill your breaks with: going on a walk, taking a nap, chatting with friends and loved ones, reading. Readers of today are the leaders of tomorrow. A reader of today builds a wealthy person for tomorrow. Reading has a way of translating people from poverty to riches. Take an annual vacation. I have not missed having an annual vacation in over 37 years of marriage with my family.

Take Advantage Of Technology That Can Help You Be More Efficient

> *In Jerusalem he (Uzziah) made machines, invented by skillful men, to be on the towers and the corners, to shoot arrows and great stones. And his fame spread far, for he was marvelously helped, till he was strong.* 2Chr 26:15

There are many tools and technologies that can help you be more efficient with your time. For example, there are apps that can help you schedule meetings, track expenses, manage to-do lists, and find time for yourself. Undock is one of these technologies. It helps make your scheduling experience more seamless by comparing your preferences and availability with others to find the optimal time. Chat GPT is an emerging AI making a world of difference. Taking advantage of these technologies will free up your time so you can focus on impactful tasks.

Learn Something New Every Day

> *Whatever you have learned or received or heard from me, or seen in me—put it into practice. And the God of peace will be with you.* Phil 4:9

It's important that you learn something new every day. This could be anything from learning a new skill, to reading a book on a topic that interests you. By constantly learning and expanding your horizon, you'll find that you have more to offer in any situation. It will also equip you with the knowledge and skills you need to accomplish your goals. You are responsible for your personal growth and productivity.

Learn how to cook, swim, pray, ski, bike, soccer, code, AI, etc. When some young members of our church come to introduce to me a new app, I ask them, are you the one that developed it? Those developing Apps are learning new things and discovering things that were not previously in existence and smiling to the bank. Learning new things can help your brain function better.

Finally, remember that it takes time to achieve outcomes and accomplish goals. Rome wasn't built in a day, and you won't see results overnight.

If you stay on course and are patient, you'll start to see improvements in your work and life, and eventually, you'll achieve the success you desire.

Manage Time

> *Behave wisely towards outsiders, making the best use of your time.* Colossian 4:5

Discover the methods that work for you. For the most part, you're the only person holding yourself accountable, so having an efficient system in place that encourages productivity and squashes procrastination is paramount. We all know that there are tons of time management techniques out there – along with countless articles and advice columns – but finding what works for you is what matters. Whether you resonate with Mark Twain's "Eat the Frog" concept, or block off your schedule into grouped tasks or prefer to keep a day a week free for focused time, what's most important is recognizing what works for you and sticking to it. My wife taught me how to use a Calendar and schedule tasks efficiently.

Understanding your productivity levels is half the battle – once you've got that figured out you can work better, be more successful and have more time to do whatever you like.

Account For How You Spend Time

You cannot invest all your time, sometimes you have to spend time. It is important to manage the time you are spending. For instance, spend time with people who inspire and motivate you. You feel more inspired and motivated to reach your goals faster. Spend time with your family. Fathers need to spend more time with their children when they are young. It's valuable to put some thought into who's in your network. These people will help you when you need it and will be a support system when you go through tough times. Invest in relationships and reap the many benefits they have to offer. You won't regret it!

1. Create a Productive Morning Routine

> *Very early in the morning, while it was still dark, He got up, went out, and made His way to a deserted place. And He was praying there.* Mk 1:35

This verse is talking about Jesus. Model your life after Jesus Christ of Nazareth. Jesus spent eighteen years from age of twelve to thirty to prepare for three and half years ministry by creating proper routine.

As they say, start the day as you mean to go on. It can be tempting to lie in bed and scroll through social media, but no matter how much you want to hit your snooze button just one more time, you shouldn't let procrastination set the tone for the rest of the day. Start your day deliberately – undertake quiet time by reading, studying, meditating on scripture powered by the Holy Ghost, get some fresh air, eat a healthy breakfast and write out your intentions for the day ahead. It might sound cliché but it works. Try Tim Ferriss' Morning Pages technique. Described by author Julia Cameron as "spiritual windshield wipers", Morning Pages give you the opportunity to scribble down all the thoughts muddying up your mind and allows you to de-clutter so you can think clearly and focus on the day ahead.

2. Set Boundaries

> *"I made a covenant with my eyes not to look with lust at a young woman."* Job 31:1

Job was telling his maid I know my boundaries. I will not crossover from my wife to my maid for any intimacy.

Part of managing your time effectively is understanding the value of your time. If you know that you work most productively during the mornings, block out time for yourself to focus on 'deep work' and refuse to answer emails, phone calls or book meetings during those hours.

Not only does this optimize your time, but it also puts an expectation in place for others around you. Jon Mackey, Managing Director at Hendricks & Struggles, refuses to take meetings on Fridays as a way of managing his schedule to ensure enough room for focused time. It may feel strange at first but once the boundary has been set, a routine will form, and people's expectations will shift.

3. Be SMART With Your Goals

> *But the plans of the Lord stand firm forever, the purposes of his heart through all generations. Psalm 33:11*

Using the SMART framework to develop achievable and relevant goals is not only useful in measuring your career success but also for deciding how you allocate your time. If you're not familiar with the concept, you want to ensure that your goals fall within the following categories:

S – Specific and significant

M – Measurable and meaningful

A – Attainable and action-oriented

R – Relevant and rewarding

T – Time-bound and track-able

Being specific is key as people are always underestimating the amount of time things take. Having clear goals and a time limit in place also helps avoid being too particular and perfectionist.

4. Delegate Or Outsource Tasks When Possible

> *"As you go into the city,"* he told them, *"you will see a certain man. Tell him, 'The Teacher says: My time has come, and I will eat the Passover meal with my disciples at your house."* Matt 26:18

Jesus outsourced the last supper. Follow his model.

Delegating tasks can be a great way to free up some of your precious time. Brian Tracey's ABCDE time management method is all about labeling a task's importance, which makes it easier when it comes to deciding what you need to prioritize. Think of it like this:

A – Most important tasks

B – Tasks with minor consequences

C – Tasks with no consequences

D – Tasks you can delegate

E – Tasks you can eliminate

Delegating tasks leaves room for the more important stuff and allows you to spend your time on jobs that have the most impact on your career.

As a portfolio professional you might want to delegate administrative tasks or outsource work you don't enjoy such as hiring an accountant to look after your finances. It may seem like an unnecessary expense, but you can't forget that your time is valuable. Use time to initiate, create, develop, build, add value to the life that exists.

Take Extreme Ownership.

> *Whatever you do, work heartily, as for the Lord and not for men, knowing that from the Lord you will receive the inheritance as your reward. You are serving the Lord Christ.* Col 3:23-24

How do you redeem time? To take ownership and control of your time; You can find inspiration and motivation from others, but you must be the one to invest your time wisely in order for it to pay off.

One way to take responsibility for your success is by taking "extreme ownership." This is a concept coined by Navy Seal Jocko Willink, and it means that you take complete responsibility for everything in your life—your work, health, relationships, etc.

When you adopt a strong attitude of ownership over your life, you have the power to make the modifications that are required to achieve success. You also develop a greater sense of self-awareness and control. As a result, you are more likely to achieve success and be more productive in both work and life.

So, if you want to be more productive and achieve greater success, invest your time wisely by taking complete responsibility for your life. Practice extreme ownership today and see how it can change your life for the better.

KEYS TO REDEEMING TIME

1. Document a plan:

For which of you, intending to build a tower, sitteth not down first, and counteth the cost, whether he have sufficient to finish it?

It is often said that those who failed to plan, planned to fail. Lack of planning means: Unnecessary actions will be taken, necessary actions may be overlooked, efficiency will be missed, opportunities will be overlooked, and risks will be unseen. You'll almost certainly have to go back and redo the work, at great expense of time and effort, because the evolved "plan" requires that. If you don't plan your day, plan your week, plan your month, or plan your years, how can you be effective? When I got to the university in 1976, I met a young man called Uzoh. He came in to study Physics. He came a year earlier and failed. His younger brother resumed with us. In Fajuyi hall in Obafemi Awolowo University, we had a Common Room where people played games and a reading room where people studied. Uzoh had a permanent seat in that reading room. He photocopied all previous exams from Prelim to final year and put it on the table. He had tons of candles and lanterns in his corner. You would constantly see Uzoh reading. Even though he failed in the first year, he was the overall best student in his graduating year in the department and in the university.

On the other hand, his brother came in to read Medicine. Now if you read the psychology of people, you will assume that someone who came in to read medicine is adjudged smarter than those admitted to read science. His brother was the first student that demonstrated magic in my presence. One day we were in the games room playing table tennis. Uzoh's brother just took the egg and it disappeared. After pleading he brought it back. Uzoh's brother had no plan for his studies. He was eventually rusticated. Joseph had plans for his future through his dreams. His brothers didn't. You know the result.

Planning involves defining your goals in writing. Making an effective action plan starts with defining and documenting. This is the way Habakkuk says it:

> [2] *And the Lord answered me, and said, Write the vision, and make it plain upon tables, that he may run that readeth it.* [3] *For the vision is yet for an appointed time, but at the end it shall speak, and not lie: though it tarry, wait for it; because it will surely come, it will not tarry.* Habakkuk 2:2-3 (KJV).

Set goals and divide the goal into milestones. Identify the resources needed. Review, reflect, and refine your documented plan.

2. **Establish your priorities**.

Create a list of tasks. Rank your tasks. Allocate time requirements for each task. Use a schedule for your day's priorities. Know when to remove tasks from your to-do list. Plan for the unexpected. Be realistic. Think backwards. Jesus was talking about prioritizing when he said:

> "*But seek ye first the kingdom of God, and his righteousness; and all these things shall be added unto you.*" Matthew 6:33 (KJV).

When God directed us to immigrate to Canada, I disobeyed God like Jonah. I brought my family and went back to Nigeria. I left my wife here with five children. Prior to coming to Canada my wife already had a master's degree in law. The oldest of our children was twelve and the youngest was three months. For her to survive from 1999 to 2001, she was doing all manner of jobs to sustain the children; of course I was supporting. It was not until

2011 that she went back and qualified as a lawyer in Canada. She devoted those years to raising the children. So many people come to Canada and misplace their priorities. All that their eyes are seeing is dollars, comparing the weight of the Canadian dollar with the weak Nigerian Naira currency. Some even at the expense of their soul will spend all their time at work and rarely find time to go to church once a week. Jesus has this to say about prioritizing your time vis-a-vis redeeming the time.

> *"For what will it profit a man if he gains the whole world, and loses his own soul?* ^{37} *Or what will a man give in exchange for his soul"* Mark 8:36-37 (NKJV).

3. Pursue Your Purpose With Passion

> *Yet preaching the Good News is not something I can boast about. I am compelled by God to do it. How terrible for me if I didn't preach the Good News!* 1Cor 9:16

> *"He(Jesus) had to go through Samaria on the way"* Jn 4:4

There is a purpose for us on earth. To redeem your time you must know what your purpose is and pursue it with passion. By His grace I am a trained engineer. I now practice Jesus engineering. I used to refine oil and now I refine souls. My calling is in the office of Evangelist and Pastoring. Paul was a trained lawyer and philosopher when God grabbed him on the way to Damascus and made him a missionary, author, and church planter. Joseph Ayo Babalola was a driver and God turned him into a worldwide evangelist. The likes of W.F Kumuyi, Pastor E. A. Adeboye were mathematics lecturers and God called them to the field of first class pastoring and teaching. Bishop David Oyedepo was a trained architect but found purpose in building one of the world's largest churches and establishing universities. These people did not just find their purpose they pursued it with passion, and they became wonders among men.

It is not over for you. I don't know your age, but you are not likely to be above eighty years old. Yet it was at the age of eighty that God called Moses. It was at seventy-five God called Abraham, so it is not about age, it is about knowing your purpose and pursuing it. Jesus told a parable of a man who hired people early in the day and in the evening he hired another set, and all of them were fully paid (Matthew 20:1-16). You don't design purpose you discover it. God design purpose for everyone. For example, the Bible says *"I knew you before I formed you in your mother's womb. Before you were born, I set you apart. and appointed you as my prophet to the nations."* Jer 1:5 Also some people discover their purpose in the morning of their life; they shine and move on- people like Dr. Martin Luther King Jr. It will interest you that John Knox began to do exploits at the age of twenty-six. Don't envy anybody, our seasons are different. Some people finish and hand over the baton to others. You are holding the baton now, don't let it fall, that is the essence of this book. Handle it properly and pass it over faithfully to the next generation.

Talking about pursuing purpose with passion, I hear how Esther and Paul, like John Knox said:

"Give me Scotland or I die."

Esther said:

"I will fast and go; if I perish I perish"

Paul said:

"But I have used none of these things, nor have I written these things that it should be done so to me; for it would be better for me to die than that anyone should make my boasting void. [16] For if I preach the gospel, I have nothing to boast of, for necessity is laid upon me; yes, woe is me if I do not preach the gospel." 1 Corinthians 9:15 -16 (NKJV).

4. Protect Your Plans And Priorities

> *So if your eye—even your good eye[k]—causes you to lust, gouge it out and throw it away. It is better for you to lose one part of your body than for your whole body to be thrown into hell* Matt 5:29

So many people crash in the pursuit of destiny. They fail to protect their priorities. The greatest and fastest way to lose and fail to redeem time is to toy with sin. Joseph protected his plan to become a leader by running away from Mrs. Potiphar. He could have been enjoying intimacy with a "sugar mummy" at the expense of becoming a Prime Minister. Samson destroyed his anointing by fondling Delilah. How many youths of our age are wasting their destinies on the laps of Delilah and on laptops watching pornography and listening to erotic, unproductive music. Their spiritual eyes have been plugged out and they are grinding pepper in correctional jails. How do you protect your priorities? Run away from temptation. Call a sin a sin. Stop giving fanciful names to sin, call a spade a spade. There are ten names we give to sin, but God calls it different names. Call sin, sin and run away from it.

i. Man calls sin an accident, God calls it an abomination.
ii. Man calls it blunder, God calls it blindness.
iii. Man calls sin defects, God calls it disease.
iv. Man calls it a chance, God calls it a choice.
v. Man calls it an error, God calls it an enmity with God.
vi. Man calls it infirmity, God calls it iniquity.
vii. Man calls it luxury, God calls it leprosy.
viii. Man calls it weakness, God calls it willfulness.
ix. Man calls it a mistake, God calls it madness.
x. Man calls it liberty, God calls it lawlessness.

Follow the principles itemized in this book to protect your time and your destiny.

5. Identify What You Value.

What are your values? Your values are the things that you believe are important in the way you live and work. Your values determine your behavior. The Christian values of today have shifted. That is the basis of God calling us to ministry. **God said to me in 2001, I have many people who profess to be Christians but are only. Christian in their mouth. Their lifestyles, which are an expression. of their values, are totally different. Therefore, go and raise an eagle generation, a generation of people that will live like genuine. Christians, a generation that will be holy and honest in their conduct, a generation of people of integrity.**

While writing this section of the book, I was reading the Book of 1st Samuel 22, and I saw how 400 people that later grew to 600 people were faithfully following David. When he was running from Saul they followed him, when he ran to live among the Philistines they followed him. I asked myself how easy it was for 600 people to follow ONE man. Remember there were no hotels in those days, even if there were hotels where was the money to fund that number of people? They were sleeping in the bush, on the grass, in the cave, and yet they were following him! Then I read at a place when in the company of Achish, a king of the Philistines and he was fighting for him against his own people! (1 Samuel 28 - 2 Samuel 2) He was loyal to whoever was his boss. He was honest. God himself called him a man after his own heart. He was hard working. Can you imagine being the eighth child in a family and you are the one tending the sheep while seven brothers are at home eating yam and pepper soup? If it were you and I, we would probably call our brothers all sorts of names. What are your values? He gave us the secret of his life when he said in Psalm 26:2-11:

> *2Examine me, O Lord, and prove me; try my reins and my heart.3For thy lovingkindness is before mine eyes: and I have walked in thy truth.4I have not sat with vain*

persons, neither will I go in with dissemblers.⁵I have hated the congregation of evil doers; and will not sit with the wicked.⁶I will wash mine hands in innocency: so will I compass thine altar, O Lord: ⁷That I may publish with the voice of thanksgiving, and tell of all thy wondrous works.⁸Lord, I have loved the habitation of thy house, and the place where thine honour dwelleth.⁹Gather not my soul with sinners, nor my life with bloody men: ¹⁰In whose hands is mischief, and their right hand is full of bribes. ¹¹But as for me, I will walk in mine integrity: redeem me, and be merciful unto me."

Friend, are you loyal to your boss? Can you be trusted? Do you defraud your office? Do you cheat on your spouse? Can your Pastor put you in the church and go to Mount Sinai and still meet the church intact?

Paul said:

"Finally, brethren, whatsoever things are true, whatsoever things are honest, whatsoever things are just, whatsoever things are pure, whatsoever things are lovely, whatsoever things are of good report; if there be any virtue, and if there be any praise, think on these things." Philippians 4:8 (KJV).

Brother and sister, may we have the right values in life in Jesus name. Let me add, don't just have great values pass the right value to your children and coming generation.

6. Make Decisions Based On Destiny.

And anyone whose name was not found recorded in the Book of Life was thrown into the lake of fire. Rev 20:15

Just like the issue of values, what drives your decision making? There are fallacies about the definition of destiny. Some believe destiny is what will be will be. If I am destined to be poor no matter how hard I work, I will die wretched. If I were to die young nobody can change it, "it is my fate" - that is a wrong way of thinking. Destiny parameters are quite different. Destiny means that there are some things you cannot change. Such as, people will be born and people will die. There is heaven and there is hell. But no one is destined to go to heaven or to hell. No one is destined to be poor. Bill Gate said "you may be born poor it is no reason to die poor." It is a function of your choices. God loves all humanity irrespective of colour, race, culture and geographical location. God does not plan for anyone to go to hell. There are two reasons Jesus has not returned to earth;

Firstly,

> *"And this gospel of the kingdom shall be preached in all the world for a witness unto all nations; and then shall the end come."* Matthew 24:14 (KJV).

And secondly,

> *"The Lord is not slack concerning his promise, as some men count slackness; but is longsuffering to us-ward, not willing that any should perish, but that all should come to repentance."* 2 Peter 3:9 (KJV).

It is good to make money but if making that money will lead you to hell then run away. If drinking alcohol shortens your life, run away from it. If abusing your spouse, especially physically, will make you lose that marriage- stop it. Are you willing to go to heaven at the end of your reign on earth? The bible says,

> *"And if thy right eye offends thee, pluck it out, and cast it from thee: for it is profitable for thee that one of thy members should perish, and not that thy whole body should be cast into hell."* Matthew 5:29 (KJV).

7. **Take Inventory of Your Associates.**

Don't join the wrong association.

> *"Be not deceived: evil communications corrupt good manners."* 1 Corinthians 15:33 (KJV).

Who are your friends, cultists or Christians? Who are your business partners? Who are your prayer partners? Who are your confidants? Where do you go to church? What are their doctrines? Where do you work? As a Chemical Engineer and a Christian are you working where they are producing alcohol even when you don't drink alcohol? If you are not yet married, take this warning seriously!

> *"Be ye not unequally yoked together with unbelievers: for what fellowship hath righteousness with unrighteousness? and what communion hath light with darkness?"* 2 Corinthians 6:14 (KJV).

Don't you know when you choose a spouse you choose where you want to spend eternity? The Yorubas have a proverb –

> *"Agutan to ba ba aja rin a je igbe"*

> *The sheep that is living in the company of dogs will eat faeces.*

> *"Never wrestle with a pig because you'll both get dirty, and the pig likes it."*

>   —George Bernard Shaw

8. **Review Your Life and Investments.**

Seek help from the right people where and when you need it. Forget the past and design your future. Paul said: *Brethren, I count not myself to have apprehended: but this one thing I do, forgetting those things which are behind, and reaching forth unto those things which are before.* Phil 3:13.

The windsheild is bigger than the rear mirror for a reason. You might have misused your past; that does not mean you must misuse your future. I went to Bogota, Colombia in May 2023. I met the President of a Pastoral Association, when we were having dinner in his church. I asked, when did you give your life? He said about thirteen years ago. Noticing that he was obviously above sixty years of age, I asked, what was your occupation before you gave your life to Christ? He shocked me, "I was in the streets for 20 years!" Now he has given his life to Christ. How many people are still on the street because they failed to review their lives? How many people's business and investments are unprofitable because they failed to review them?

9. **Do Not Try To Please Everyone.**

> *For I came down from heaven, not to do mine own will, but the will of him that sent me.* John 6:38.

Most people's life is about seeking other people's approval. Their dressing is to impress and please others. They don't do business that God gives them direction to do, rather they copy their colleagues. They saw the cement business moving and opened their shop selling cement. When they sing in church, it is to impress the crowd rather than to give glory to God. Pastors preach to please the congregation so that they will contribute financially and also remain in the church. Whether the people are born again or going to hell is irrelevant?

> *"Friends, For what shall it profit a man, if he shall gain the whole world, and lose his own soul? [37] Or what shall a man give in exchange for his soul?"* Mk 8:36-38

My counsel, be like the Master, the Lord Jesus Christ who pleased only his father in heaven, decide to please only one person, the Lord Jesus Christ your Maker. That is what will guarantee you success in business, marriage, career and ministry and at the end make heaven.

Hear what Jesus told Peter when he left all and resolved to please Jesus with his life. Mk 10:28-31.

> *Peter began to tell Him, "Look, we have left everything and followed You." ²⁹"I assure you," Jesus said, "there is no one who has left house, brothers or sisters, mother or father,[j] children, or fields because of Me and the gospel, ³⁰who will not receive 100 times more, now at this time—houses, brothers and sisters, mothers and children, and fields, with persecutions—and eternal life in the age to come. ³¹But many who are first will be last, and the last first."*

It's not enough to be busy, so are the ants.
The question is, what are we busy about?
—Henry David Thoreau

Watch your thoughts, they become your words; watch
your words, they become your actions; watch your actions,
they become your habits; watch your habits, they become your
character; watch your character, it becomes your destiny.
—Anonymous

For "Everyone who calls on the name of the Lord will be saved."
—Paul

And anyone whose name was not found recorded
in the Book of Life was thrown into the lake of fire.
—John The Beloved

CHAPTER THREE

THE ACRONYMS OF REDEEMING TIME

Since the inception of our International Gathering of Eagle Conferences in Toronto, I make a presentation on the Friday night of the four-day event that runs from Thursday through Sunday of the third week of September. God gives me revelation on how to communicate the theme of the conference as an ACRONYM. Below is the one God gave me during the 2016 conference, the acronym of R-E-D-E-E-M-I-N-G and T-I-M-E:

R-Redeem

R- Redeem your soul before you can redeem anything else. Your soul has to be redeemed before you can redeem time. If you fail to redeem your soul, you cannot redeem your time appropriately. 3 John 2. The only reason Jesus came is to redeem mankind from sin and destruction in hell.

If you have not accepted Christ, now is the time

> *"for He says, "At the acceptable time (kairos = the opportune time!) I listened to you, and on the day of salvation I will help you"; behold, now is "The acceptable time (kairos)," behold, now is "The day of salvation"* 2 Corinthians 6:2 .

If you use all your time on earth to build houses, make money, pursue fame and do not know Jesus as Lord and savior I can tell you categorically that such life is being wasted. Redeem your life now accept Jesus as Lord and Saviour.

E- Essence is to Glorify God

E-essence of redeeming time is to glorify God and fulfill destiny or purpose. Redeeming time is not just to spend life on earth as a Methuselah. If all the years you spend on earth are not to glorify God or advance God's (your creator) purpose you have abused the space you occupied on earth.

Psalm 90:12, How do you glorify God? By living a life of holiness, righteousness and integrity. God is much more concerned about your character than your career, because your character will determine whether you will go to eternity with Jesus. Do people glorify God because of your lifestyle?

D-Delay Not

D-Delay can be dangerous. Many of us live a life of regret because we specialize in procrastination. As mentioned above - once an opportunity is lost you may never regain it. (Read my book-Dream Dreams and Have Dominion, especially Chapter Three, subtitled - Do It)

Whatever you need to do right now, do it. Start that business, read that bible, pray that prayer, make that call, send that email, register for that course. Go to that university for the first degree. If need be, go for the Masters. then go for your doctorate. Go to that service, give that offering/gift, help that neighbor now. Read that book, write that book, go on that mission trip. Prepare to attend the next International Gathering of Eagles Conference. Register today to attend that Eagle Academy course.

E-Environment

E- Environment should not determine how you spend your time but godly guidance: Take for instance God wants you to live in Africa and you say by force and by fire you will live in Canada. See how environment affected Abraham and Lot.

Abraham in Genesis 12 saw prosperity in Egypt, because there was famine in Canaan, he jumped without asking God. He compromised his integrity. He abused his wife emotionally! It took God's intervention for Pharaoh not to sleep with Abraham's wife in Egypt. The most devastating effect of that environmental factor is that in Egypt he met Hagar who gave birth to Ishmael and like they say the rest is history.

The catastrophe and calamity Abraham brought to humanity remains forever. Imagine if Abraham did not go to Egypt, there would be no ISIS, Hezbollah, Al- Qaeda, Al- Shaaban, Boko haram.

Lot saw a land plain well-watered, and he did not allow his uncle to choose first. Where did it land him? It landed him in the land of Sodom and Gomorrah, the land of Sodomy, there we first heard about homosexuality!

Is that not what brought many of us to the western world? We looked like Lot, we saw a well-watered western world, constant power supply, good roads, nice buildings and today we have found ourselves in the land of Sodom.

This is the way a sticker puts it.

> *"When I came here same sex marriage was illegal, then it became acceptable, them it became legal, should I not leave before it becomes compulsory?"*

E-Evaluate

E- evaluate how you are spending your time now before it is too late. Redeeming your time is about evaluation of your time. We are products of our past, but we don't have to be prisoners of it. It reminds me of the story of the professor and the student. The professor gave an assignment to a student, he completed the assignment and the professor marked it. Research - excellent, presentation- excellent, Grade - F. The student protested. The professor said, "man, you did the wrong assignment." The millennia are speeding, and the return of Jesus Christ is fast approaching.

How many souls have you won for Christ? How many projects have you executed for God? How many people have you prayed for? How many people have you reconciled to God? What percentage of your income do you give to advance the kingdom? How many orphans have you taken care of? If you die today, what will you be remembered for? Don't just kill time, redeem it. Don't just spend time, invest it in a worthwhile venture. Don't just count time, make the days count. Time will not tell just anything; Time will tell what you have done, good or bad!

M-Maximize Time

M- maximize your life. Your life is too precious to be wasted. Make that your goal. People struggle with time management. The secret of managing your time effectively is to know what you want to do and when you want to do it. Have a plan for an immediate goal, middle life goal and long term goals and be committed to doing it. We become what we are committed to.

Have a purpose. What is your purpose? If you don't know where you are going people will push you down. If you don't stand for something, you will fall for everything. Are you a jack of all trades and master of nothing?

I –Innovate/Invent

Be an innovator. Be an inventor. So many things have been invented, but we are still at the periphery of what will be invented by human beings. There is surely no limit to human imagination, and the resources of God under the earth and the ocean are so vast that once those items are invented, they can be manufactured easily. Recently, I saw a bus that was driven on land and later on water, before I could catch my breath I saw a car driven on land then driven over the sea and flew using the water as the take off route! What are you using your gray matter or *medulla oblongat*a for!

What does it mean to innovate/invent? To me it means to use your God given time and talent to solve human problems and make yourself rich in the process.

1. Thomas Edison is one of the most significant innovators and inventors in American history. Edison is perhaps best known for inventing the first long-lasting, commercially practical incandescent light bulb. I read a very interesting story about Edison. One day he came home with a note from the teacher to the mother. The mother said with tears in her eyes "your teacher wrote your son is a genius this school is too small for him. We don't have teachers who can train him, please teach him yourself." That is what the mother did. Many years later when the mother had gone to be with the Lord, he found the old paper he gave the mother. He was surprised about the content "your son is mentally ill we won't let him come to school any more" Edison realized what the mother has done for him. What are you doing for your children and the people around you?

2. Steve Jobs. The iconic American entrepreneur and founder of Apple will go down in history as one of the great innovators of our time. He invented the iPod, iPhone, and iPad.

3. Nikola Tesla, a great inventor, engineer, and futurist, Tesla helped develop the Alternating Current electrical delivery system. This electric vehicle has been designed to meet modern needs in a fanciful way by Elon Musk.

4. Bill Gates, One of the greatest businessman/philanthropists of the last century, Microsoft guru.

5. Benjamin Franklin. One of the founding fathers of the United States, Franklin was a brilliant polymath, inventor, political theorist, scientist, statesman, and writer. Best known for his experiments with lightning and electricity.

6. Leonardo Da Vinci. The original "Renaissance man," Da Vinci is best known for his dramatic and expressive artwork.

7. Alexander Graham Bell. A Scottish inventor and engineer, a telecommunications, aeronautics guru. Bell was awarded the US patent for the telephone in 1876.

8. Sandford Fleming. A Scottish-Canadian innovator and inventor, Fleming used his engineering, surveying, and mapmaking skills to help build the transcontinental railways of the nineteenth century. He was also the inventor of worldwide standard time and the standard time zones used today.

9. Marie Curie. The first female winner of the Nobel Prize in 1903 (she won it twice in both physics and chemistry), Curie was a pioneering physicist and chemist who is known for her breakthrough ideas in radioactivity and her discovery of two elements.

10. The Wright brothers. Orville & Wilbur Wright invented and flew the world's first successful airplane in 1903. Their persistence, experimentation, and work on the principles of flight made them legendary inventors and innovators.

Spiritual Inventors

Below are some people that I refer to as ***Spiritual inventors.*** Since an inventor is one who, alone or with others, first invents a new and useful process, machine, composition of matter, or other patentable subject matter. The most important consideration in determining inventorship is the initial conception of the invention. These spiritual inventors may not have a number in the archives of the United States of America or Canada but surely have their patents and articles written in the heavenly book. They labored hard to transform the lives of men through prayers.

Joseph Seymor (May 2, 1870 – September 28, 1922). This is what Wikipedia reports about him. He was an African-American holiness preacher who initiated (invented, my idea) the Azusa Street Revival, an influential event in the rise of the Pentecostal and Charismatic movements. The revival acted as a catalyst for the spread of Pentecostal practices, such as speaking in tongues and integrated worship, throughout the world. It also played an important role in the history of most major Pentecostal denominations.

John Knox- (1514 – 24 November 1572) He was a Scottish minister, Reformed theologian, and writer who was a leader of the country's Reformation. He was the founder of the Presbyterian Church of Scotland. The prayer "Give me Scotland or I die" famously came from the lips of John Knox, the Scottish reformer. God used Knox to bring about the reformation of the church and the transformation of the nation. God is desiring to see young men and women today who will pray and not play away their time. Who will pray and change the new face of England where the "churches are dead." As at the time I am writing this book, the Prime Minister of Britain, Rishi Sunak is the first British Asian and Hindu to hold the office of prime minister. The church neglected their God as the ten tribes of Israel.

In 1996 I was privileged to preach in Church of England in Manchester- I was told the whole service cannot be more than one hour and the sermon time allocated to me was fifteen minutes. With me from Africa around that time my minimum sermon time was **one hour**- I found it very strange. So I appealed to them to give me more time. After two evening meetings with the woman vicar in-charge they gave me thirty minutes. The first day I attended the service there were less than thirty people in a cathedral building that can seat two hundred people comfortably. Apparently with the announcement that an African pastor was coming to a largely Caucasian church the attendance that day increased to about fifty people. Out of all that attended only the Vicar and I were obviously under fifty years old! Though I challenged them during my message by asking – Where are your youth? Where are the people to take over from you? The lack of youth in the church of England and the continuous selling of the cathedrals to their rival religions Muslims, Hindus, Buddhists and to cinemas/theaters and club houses led to this state of quagmire the church of England has found itself in. The solution can only come from radical evangelism, aggressive intercession of prayer similar if not more intense than that of John Knox.

Joseph Ayodele Babalola- (1904- 1959) He is credited as the Revivalist and founder of Christ Apostolic Church based on the way God used him especially in 1930 when God raised a dead person through him which led to a worldwide crusade at Oke-Oye in Ilesha in the South West part of Nigeria. He was known to be a prayer machine that witches and wizards feared. He planted churches in dangerous forests.

Here are three of his famous quotations.

> *"Knowing is not enough; we must apply. Wishing is not enough; we must do"*

> *"The pessimist sees difficulty in every opportunity. The optimist sees opportunity in every difficulty."*

> *"When you tell the truth, the world may take away earthly benefits from you but cannot take eternal benefits from you"*

Pa Josiah Akindayomi (1909- 1980) Could be credited as an inventor of The Redeemed Christian Church of God. Reverend Akindayomi chose Pastor Enoch Adejare Adeboye as the next General Overseer, a mathematics lecturer from University of Lagos. In 2008, it had 14,000 churches in 80 countries and five million members in Nigeria alone.

IGOE- Amos Dele Dada (1955-date) He is by the grace of God the inventor of International Gathering of Eagles Conferences. Started pastoring at the age of 30 in 1985 by planting Christ Apostolic Church Bethel, Effurun Warri. In 2001 he emigrated to Canada fully and invented IGOE in 2003. God told him to raise an eagle generation, a people of holiness, power and integrity and to put Canada on the spiritual map of the world. He has held this leadership conference across five continents and 45 nations including China, South Korea, Senegal Thailand, Singapore, and many African nations.

What are you waiting for- Go and invent something that this generation and the coming generation can benefit from. Start that company, start that church/ministry, write that book, develop that App.

N-No

No is a good word

No to the devil

No to sin.

No to time wasters/wasting/mismanagement.

No to wrong association,

No to anger, hatred, wickedness.

No to addictions, womanizing, adultery, fornication, cigarette smoking, alcoholism, terrorism, cocaine, pornography, rape, assaults, masturbation, New Age Movement, and LGBTQ2(Gal 5:19-21)

No is a good word. Learn to say no to what is evil. No to the devil. No to the wrong company. No to failure. No to Limitation. No to evil thoughts and imaginations.

G-God will judge the world.

G- God will judge how you spend your time.

> *"For he has set a day when he will judge the world with justice by the man he has appointed. He has given proof of this to everyone by raising him from the dead."* Acts 17:31 (NIV).

> *"He commanded us to preach to the people and to testify that he is the one whom God appointed as judge of the living and the dead."* Acts 10:42 (NIV).

Take Time.

Your time—and how you use it—is important.

Examine your schedule. Learn to budget your time and manage it well.

Take time to work—it is the price of success.

Take time to think—it is the source of power.

Take time to play—it is the secret of youth.

Take time to read—it is the foundation of knowledge.

Take time to worship—it is the highway of reverence for God and mechanism for life relief.

Take time to help and enjoy family, friends, church members- it is the source of happiness.

Take time to love—it is the one sacrament of life.

Take time to dream—it hitches the soul to the stars.

Take time to laugh—it is the music of the soul.

Take time to pray—it helps bring Christ near.

Take time to win souls - It is one of the great reasons God has kept you on planet earth.

Acronym of T-I-M-E

T - Today

T - Today is what you have, tomorrow is not secured. Jesus says there are 12 hours that we have to work the night cometh when no one can work. Stop worrying about tomorrow and stop waiting for tomorrow. Prepare for tomorrow today. Tomorrow will come or may not come. Give God today, and He will take care of tomorrow. Yesterday is past, tomorrow is a mystery- what you have is today, redeem the time. The rich fool had a plan to build a bigger barn, but Jesus said-

> *"Thou fool- this night I will require your soul"* Luke 12:20.

> *"Take therefore no thought for the morrow: for the morrow shall take thought for the things of itself. Sufficient unto the day is the evil thereof."* Matt 6:34

Richard Brainerd said-

> *"It is too late to redeem the time that is past, but not the time that is passing."*

Purpose to do something from today.

You can abolish the modern day slave trade (Human trafficking, addictions etc) again, you can do the impossible!

Young William Wilberforce was discouraged one night in the early 1790s after another defeat in his ten-year battle against the slave trade in England. Tired and frustrated, he opened his Bible and began to leaf through it. A small piece of paper fell out and fluttered to the floor. It was a letter written by John Wesley shortly before his death.

Wilberforce read it again:

> *"Unless the divine power has raised you up... I see not how you can go through your glorious enterprise in opposing that (abominable practice of slavery), which is the scandal of religion, of England, and of human nature. Unless God has raised you up for this very thing, you will be worn out by the opposition of men and devils. But If God be for you, who can be against you? Are all of them together stronger than God? Oh, be not weary of well-doing. Go on in the name of God, and in the power of his might."*

William Wilberforce worked hard and on the first day of January 1808, a new Federal law made it illegal to import captive people from Africa into the United States. This date marks the end—the permanent, legal closure—of the trans-Atlantic slave trade. You are the William Wilberforce of this generation, discover what you are to fight for or fight against.

Moses was passionate about delivering the Israelites from Egypt; he achieved his aim. Are you to fight abortion? Racial profiling? I have two things that I am fighting globally, firstly in Africa, corruption. Corruption among the leaders of Africa with 54 countries and over 750 million people impoverished. In 2014, I wrote a book titled "To The Rescue (Say No To Corruption)." This is a fictional novel that can help the youth to understand the concept of endemic corruption and to stand against it. The book is geared towards being used in high schools and tertiary institutions as a moral guide and could be undertaken as a General Knowledge Study (GKS) especially in tertiary institutions.

The second thing I am passionate about, like William Wilberforce, is that I am fighting for Canada to see biblical education restored to Canadian Schools. There is a framed newspaper picture on my wall in my office that reads, "Pastor advocates returning Bible to Schools" -that is my passion. We are in the age where government officials with liberal ideology are bent on changing the school education curriculum to promote same-sex agenda. This is another modern-day "slave trade" to force the coming generation as they did to the young Africans to a journey of mental, unbiblical, unnatural ideology and lifestyle - this must not be allowed to stand.

Everyone is born a leader but what makes you a leader is the ability to discover your purpose and pursue it with all it takes to liberate humanity from satanic controls. While holding International Gathering of Eagles in Conference in Sweden 2017 God spoke to me to return to Canada and start what is called Canada Return To Your Maker Prayer Summit we started in 2018.

I - Invite

I - Invite people to Jesus. That is your purpose. Go and proclaim Jesus with your time. Use your time to get someone to eternity. For example:

1. Ask your waiter if there is anything you can pray for him (her) about when you pray over your meal. You will be surprised at the variety of responses, some of which will open a door for the gospel to be shared! Deliberately forget a tract in a public place or vehicle. The concept is whatever is written will be read. Do whatever it will take to invite someone to Jesus.

2. When you get one of those irritating cold calls soliciting for money or something else, turn it into an opportunity to ask your caller if they know Jesus as Savior. Beside, it is interesting how the number of calls decrease! Great opportunities may come once in a lifetime, but small opportunities surround us every day."

3. Pray daily for an unreached people group, your neighbours, colleagues, family members that are yet to know Jesus Christ. Let us not just "mark time," but use time to make our mark! Yes, time flies, but remember that you are the "navigator!"

M - Money

M - Money is good. You need money to live. The gospel needs money to be preached, we all make money and spend money. The big question is how you make money and how you spend it? If you make money in an ungodly way, trouble erupts, if you spend it in an ungodly way that is more trouble. What is the message in redeeming the time? How you make money and spend it must conform to God's standard and help you on your trip to eternity.

> *"Wealth [not earned but] won in haste or unjustly or from the production of things for vain or detrimental use [such riches] will dwindle away, but he who gathers little by little will increase [his riches] Proverbs 13:11 (AMPC)*

E - Eternity

E - Eternity with God must be your goal, must be your focus, must be your preoccupation from today. As you leave this place ask yourself, if I die today will I make heaven? That is how you can count your days. That is how you can redeem your time.

*In my Father's house are many mansions: if it were not so, I would have told you. I am going to prepare a place for you. **3** And if I go and prepare a place for you, I will come again, and receive you unto myself; that where I am, there ye may be also.* John 14:2-3

If your T of Time has no eternal value, it is a waste!

Principles Versus Principalities

Where principalities are working, principles may not work! This book is about principles. Principles are great as a guide for helping us to navigate the complexities life throws at us. In studying the Bible there are things you come across, history, promises, commands, prophecies fulfilled and yet to be fulfilled, the rest are principles to guide our lives. But much as we want to use these principles to help our lives it is important to remind you that principalities work very hard to frustrate principles.

Paul said,

> *"For our struggle is not against flesh and blood, but against the rulers, against the authorities, against the powers of this dark world and against the spiritual forces of evil in the heavenly realms. ¹³Therefore put on the full armor of God, so that when the day of evil comes, you may be able to stand your ground, and after you have done everything, to stand. ¹⁴Stand firm then, with the belt of truth buckled around your waist, with the breastplate of righteousness in place, ¹⁵and with your feet fitted with the readiness that comes from the gospel of peace. ¹⁶In addition to all this, take up the shield of faith, with which you can extinguish all the flaming arrows of the evil one. ¹⁷Take the helmet of salvation and the sword of the Spirit, which is the word of God. ¹⁸And pray in the Spirit on all occasions with all kinds of prayers and requests. With this in mind, be alert*

and always keep on praying for all the Lord's people. ^{19}*Pray also for me, that whenever I speak, words may be given me so that I will fearlessly make known the mystery of the gospel,* ^{20}*for which I am an ambassador in chains. Pray that I may declare it fearlessly, as I should."* Ephesians 6:12-20 (NIV).

The only way to achieve the wonderful objectives of this book is to read, put it in practice and **pray it to action.**

Rewrite Your History

It is not too late to redeem the time when you are still alive.

Decide now what you want written on your tombstone, then live your life backwards from there. Life is short and ought to be taken seriously. Decide now how you would like to be remembered, then live your life accordingly. If your activities don't match your priorities, you are wasting your life." "Never let an impossible situation intimidate you. Let it motivate you – to pray more, trust more, work harder, expect more." Do you want your tombstone to read, "He was the head of his corporation," or, "She was the best in her field"? Or would you rather it reflects an important contribution you've made to life? If, at the end of your life, you want to say, "I did," instead of "I wish," alter your course. today.

The story of Alfred Nobel.

Swedish chemist Alfred Nobel awoke one morning and read his own obituary in the local newspaper. It read, "Alfred Nobel, the inventor of dynamite, who died yesterday, devised a way for more people to be killed in a war than ever before, and he died a very rich man." Actually, it was Alfred's older brother who had died; a newspaper reporter had bungled the epitaph. But that account had a tremendous impact on Nobel, who decided he wanted to be remembered for something different. As a result, he initiated the Nobel Prize to reward individuals who foster peace. He said,

> "Every man ought to have a chance to correct his epitaph in midstream and write a new one."

Today you have the opportunity to start working on what you want to be remembered for. I listen to Evangelist Reinhard Bonke, a man God used tremendously to save millions of souls in Africa - He said they should write three words on his epitaph for him:

> "He preached Jesus".

What do you want written on your epitaph?

Let this book be the catalyst and game changer to your life!

Time to Prophesy

I prophesy to you

You will redeem your time.

You will rewrite your history.

You will be Born Again.

You will live long and serve God.

You shall pursue and recover all the years you have wasted.

You will live in good health.

You will never lose or bury your children.

I pray that all the children and youth that are under the sound of my voice that have misused their life and time will recover it.

To you parents, I decree and declare that nobody will stand for you on the day of your children's celebration.

Your position will not be vacant when your children are graduating and having their wedding and doing great things.

When you call on money, it will answer you.

Prophecy Galore

You will have money to spend in life and in this generation. You will not beg for bread.

You yourself will not rest on your oars. You are too young to be complacent, you will rise to prominent positions in your generation.

You will develop yourself in the name of Jesus.

You will not become a widow and your husband will not become a widower.

Pastor, your desire over your calling and ministry shall be accomplished.

Pastor, you will not lose your wife and children in the course of ministry.

Sickness and diseases will not cut short your life, ministry and calling in Jesus name.

You will succeed beyond your dreams. You will not retire, you will refire. You shall become a soul winner, leading many to Christ, redeeming souls.

You will overtake your contemporaries, competitors, and your colleagues.

Whether the devil likes it or not, you Shall REDEEM YOUR TIME IN JESUS NAME.

INTERNATIONAL Gathering of Eagles CONFERENCE 2016

SEPTEMBER 15-18, 2016

CHRIST APOSTOLIC CHURCH
BETHEL TORONTO

22-94 KENHAR DR.
TORONTO ON, M9L 1N2

T: 647-430-8936 | CEL: 416-616-2425
IGOECAC@GMAIL.COM

JOIN US AS WE REACH CANADA AND BEYOND WITH THE GOSPEL!

COME AND EXPERIENCE SALVATION, RESTORATION, DELIVERANCE, HEALING, IMPARTATION, AND MORE.

WWW.CACBETHEL.COM

PASTOR & LADY EVANG. AMOS DADA
CONFERENCE CONVENERS

• **SPECIAL FEATURES** •

SCHOOL OF MINISTRY:
FRIDAY & SATURDAY
10:30am-3:30pm

EVENING SESSIONS:
THURSDAY, FRIDAY, & SATURDAY - 7pm

SUNDAY SERVICE: 10:00am

THEME
REDEEMING THE TIMES

FEATURED GUEST MINISTERS

 REV. REGGIE ABRAHAM — INDIA
 REV. JUDY MAYES — USA
 REV. SAMUEL SOWAH — GHANA
 BISHOP AUDLEY JAMES — CANADA

GOSPEL ARTISTS

 KEVIN — NIGERIA
 LADY EVANG. TOYIN DADA — CANADA

REGISTER TODAY AT WWW.IGOEMINISTRY.COM

Books by Pastor Dada

- 1. To The Rescue-Say No To Corruption
- 2. The Way Forward
- 3. What Is Faith
- 4. Dream Dreams and Have Dominion
- 5. Turning Curses To Blessing
- 6. Destroying Curse and Evil Covenant
- 7. Making The Church Relevant To The Society
- 8. Understanding Principles, Purpose, Power and People of Vision
- 9. Discipling Nations
- 10. The Gates of Hell Shall Not Prevail.
- 11. What The Holy Spirit Taught Me This Morning
- 12. Canada Return To Your Maker

To order these books contact:

www.cacbethel.com
www.igoeministry.com
www.amosdada.com

amos.dada@gmail.com
Cell: 4166162425
6474308936

To order any of these books,
contact the author or go online.

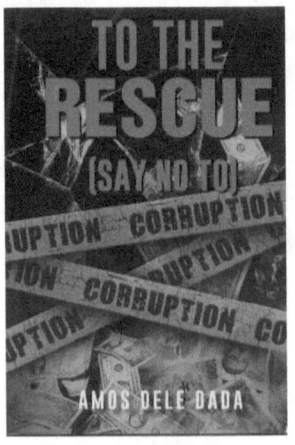

To order any of these books,
contact the author or go online or pick during convention.

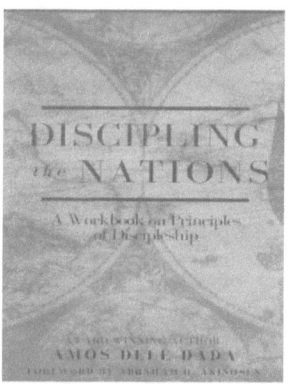

www.ingramcontent.com/pod-product-compliance
Lightning Source LLC
Chambersburg PA
CBHW060408080526
44583CB00012B/510